The Teacher's

Daily

Helper

*Daily Meditations
for Teachers*

Jon W. Tice

Providence
PUBLICATIONS
KOKOMO · INDIANA

"Thy Word is a lamp unto my feet,
and a light unto my path."

Presented

To: _____

By: _____

Date: _____, _____

First Printing 1999

ISBN 0-9671383-0-2

Visit Our Website At:
www.providencepubl.com

PUBLICATIONS
KOKOMO • INDIANA

Printed in the United States of America.

Dedicated to...

My parents who taught me the fundamentals.
My teachers who taught me to focus.
My wife who teaches me to be free.
My little girl who teaches me to have fun.

Acknowledgements

Every person who accomplishes anything in life always does so because other people have invested in them.
Special thanks to all my teachers, coaches, and friends who have invested in me to help make this book a reality.
Thanks to Peggy Brubaker, Don Criss, Frances Flora, Janet Hanna, Roberta Lineback, Judy Rausch and my dad and mom, Don and Margaret Tice, all who have devoted themselves to teaching others.
They gave me valuable feedback and helped edit this manuscript.
Thanks also to Scott Whitten, who once again used his creativity to help me communicate.
Special thanks to my partner in ministry and my friend, Dan Johnson.
Finally, thanks to my wife, Stacey, and my daughter, Abby, for their daily support and ongoing love.

Welcome

Christian School Teachers

There are no utopias on this green earth. You have the unique privilege to minister in a place that enables you to keep a Bible on your desk, to open it every day and to say to your students, "This is what God says about . . . ." Let me encourage you to maximize this wonderful privilege by using that privilege freely. In most Christian schools there are morning devotions led by the teacher. *The Teacher's Daily Helper* was written with that context in mind.

Allow me to suggest that you use the weekly theme and the daily verse for personal enrichment and then as a springboard into your daily challenge to your students. If you send a weekly note home to parents you can let them know of the theme for that week as well. It is my hope to encourage you in the vital ministry of teaching God's truth.

Public School Teachers

If you are a Christian teacher in a public school, you are in a great place for ministry. The spiritual needs are great and the opportunity for the truth to be clearly seen is incredible.

Let me remind you the greater the darkness, the more easily displayed is a vibrant life. Jesus said in the Sermon on the Mount, "You are the light of the world. A city on a hill cannot be hidden. Neither do people light a lamp and put it under a bowl. Instead they put it on its stand, and it gives light to everyone in the house. In the same way, let your light shine before men, that they may see your good deeds and praise your Father in heaven" (Matthew 5:14-16). If you are a Christian in a public school, the hope that you display, the love that you give, the faith that you hold will express itself through your life. *The Teacher's Daily Helper* was written to encourage your heart. As you use this tool each day allow me to suggest that you paraphrase the concepts from the prayer and use them as a "Thought for the Day" in your classroom: You will not need to give a Bible reference and yet the truth will still be displayed. If we can quote Henry David Thoreau and William James, we certainly can quote the best selling book of all time: the Bible.

Home-School Teachers

All parents are teachers, but you have embarked on not only teaching the lessons of life but on teaching the academic facts of life as well. Congratulations! Your task is not easy, but as you well know it is very rewarding. To see the "light come on" may be more rewarding for the home schooling teacher than it is for the home schooling child.

Allow me to suggest using the weekly theme and verses as part of your personal preparation for your teaching day. The intentional briefness was designed with you in mind. These themes and verses could also be used as part of your devotional time as class begins each day. Verses that tie into your Bible curriculum can be highlighted for memory work.

It was my hope that *The Teacher's Daily Helper* would be another usable tool so that you can continue to help your children be prepared for the race of living a life for God.

Sunday School Teachers

The Sunday school as we have come to know it had its roots in England in the early 1800's to teach street children how to read so they could understand the Bible. Since that time multiplied thousands of children have come to know the simple message of salvation in Jesus Christ through the influence of faithful Sunday school teachers. The power in any teaching about God and His word comes through individual teachers who are themselves in a growing, dynamic relationship with Jesus Christ. The tools God has entrusted us with are prayer and the Bible.

It is my desire to encourage all teachers and especially Sunday school teachers, to use *The Teacher's Daily Helper* to build your heart through the personal disciplines of prayer and meditation on God's word. Use it each week in your own preparation and take some of those lessons on each theme to your Sunday school class each week.

Contents

Forward

Teaching is such a rewarding experience. What a thrill it is watching children learn, receiving hugs, and observing the great energy and enthusiasm of children. Teaching is also an awesome responsibility. What we do today shapes tomorrow! With the increased number of family problems in our society, teachers assume even more responsibility for helping children. Many of the social ills have to be met before the child can learn. The teacher receives help by asking God for direction each day and praying for specific individuals.

Jon, with the support of his wife, Stacey and their daughter, Abby, has given teachers a tool to use for short times of prayer and Scripture meditation each day. He has taught school and has volunteered in my classroom. I have observed his love for children and his passion for helping others. Jon knows first hand the many needs that children have and is doing his best to help teachers help children.

This book is for teachers, but we are all teachers. Whether you are a parent, a grandparent, aunt, uncle, or a friend of a child, you are a teacher. Many times adults never realize the impact that they make on children. This book may be for you.

There is such power in prayer! With God's help we can each make a difference. If each person, using prayer and The Word, helps one or two children, we can make tomorrow better.

Frances Flora
29 years teaching elementary
Northwestern School Corporation
March 1999

How to Use This Tool

Teaching is the power to impact a life forever. Thankfully, Jesus, the greatest teacher who ever lived, modeled teaching in a variety of ways so that those of us who are endeavoring to teach others might have hope. His life showed us that life-changing teaching is rarely evident until many years after the students are gone. The harsh reality for many of us who teach others is that our students rarely remember the facts that we sought to teach them. What they do remember is the daily visiblity of a life well lived. Students catch more, usable life-truth by the way we live than they learn by the words we say. One life influencing a few other lives is the way that we change the world. My hope and prayer is that you share that belief with me. This resource was developed to touch you so that you can touch your world.

This year-long guide was created so that in 2 to 5 minutes a day through the disciplines of prayer and meditation on the Word you may be called to focus on the teacher's real daily helper: God.

This tool was designed from school beginning to school beginning. May I recommend the following pattern for its use:

1. Pray the prayer every day for a week adding your own heartfelt thoughts and prayers as you go.

2. Meditate on the verse for each day.

3. Communicate these thoughts into the life lessons that you and your students need for vibrant, dynamic, strategic, exciting living.

4. Record significant life lessons in "Reflections."

Jim W. Fite

March 1999

Week 1

Review

Lord, review and repetition is the life of a teacher. Many of the lessons that were learned last year have already become a faded memory. My desire is to creatively resurrect those thoughts and retrain the mind where it didn't capture facts correctly. Frequently, You use the experiences in my life to help me recall the lessons that you have been teaching me for such a long time. Thank You for Your patience with my review. Today, help me to seize every opportunity to call to each student's mind the beauty of learning. May Your patience with me remind me of how to patiently work with my students today.

Day 1

Dear friends, this is now my second letter to you. I have written both of them as reminders to stimulate you to wholesome thinking. I want you to recall the words spoken in the past by the holy prophets and the command given by our Lord and Savior through your apostles. -2 Peter 3:1,2

Day 2

Hear, O Israel: The LORD our God, the LORD is one. Love the LORD your God with all your heart and with all your soul and with all your strength. These commandments that I give you today are to be upon your hearts. Impress them on your children. Talk about them when you sit at home and when you walk along the road, when you lie down and when you get up.
-Deuteronomy 6:4-7

Day 3

Tie them as symbols on your hands and bind them on your foreheads. Write them on the door frames of your houses and on your gates. When the LORD your God brings you into the land He swore to your fathers, to Abraham, Isaac and Jacob, to give you—a land with large, flourishing cities you did not build, houses filled with all kinds of good things you did not provide, wells you did not dig, and vineyards and olive groves you did not plant—then when you eat and are satisfied, be careful that you do not forget the LORD, who brought you out of Egypt, out of the land of slavery. -Deuteronomy 6:8-12

Day 4

Whom shall he teach knowledge? And whom shall he make to understand doctrine? Them that are weaned from the milk, and drawn from the breasts. For precept must be upon precept, precept upon precept; line upon line, line upon line; here a little, and there a little: -Isaiah 28:9-10 (KJV)

Day 5

My child, keep your father's commands and do not forsake your mother's teaching. Bind them upon your heart forever; fasten them around your neck. When you walk, they will guide you; when you sleep, they will watch over you; when you awake, they will speak to you. For these commands are a lamp, this teaching is a light, and the corrections of discipline are the way to life.

-Proverbs 6:20-23

Reflections through the week

_____

_____

_____

_____

_____

_____

_____

_____

_____

_____

Week 2

Hope

*Lord, help my words and actions to bring positive anticipation
of the potential of today.
Lord, You know how each student today needs a special
touch from You. Please make each child's need clear to me so
that I may be Your Hands to touch that child for You.
Thank You for letting me teach! Today, may my teaching
show my world what You are teaching me.*

Day 1

Be strong and take heart, all you who hope in the Lord.
-Psalm 31:24

Day 2

But the eyes of the LORD are on those who fear him,
on those whose hope is in his unfailing love.
-Psalm 33:18

Day 3

We wait in hope for the Lord; he is our help and our shield.
May your unfailing love rest upon us,
O Lord, even as we put our hope in you.
-Psalm 33:20,22

Day 4

Why are you downcast, O my soul? Why so disturbed within me? Put
your hope in God, for I will yet praise him, my Savior and my God.
-Psalm 42:5

Day 5

Be joyful in hope, patient in affliction, faithful in prayer.
-Romans 12:12

Reflections through the week

_____

_____

_____

_____

_____

_____

_____

_____

_____

_____

Week 3

Children

Dear Father, thank You for letting me be Your child. Not all the children whom I will teach today know what it means to have a parent who is "there" for them. Although I can not take the place of that parent, Lord, I know that I can serve with a heart full of love for them. Today, may I remember that You have been the perfect parent to me. Although You are sometimes mysterious, You can always be trusted. I trust You with the lives of these students today. You always do what is best, even when things look the worst. I trust You again, today!

Day 1

I rescued the poor who cried for help,
and the fatherless who had none to assist him. -Job 29:12

Day 2

But you, O God, do see trouble and grief;
you consider it to take it in hand. The victim commits himself to you;
You are the helper of the fatherless. -Psalm 10:14

Day 3

Therefore, whoever humbles himself like this child
is the greatest in the kingdom of heaven. And whoever welcomes a
little child like this in my name welcomes me. -Matthew 18:4,5

Day 4

You hear, O Lord, the desire of the afflicted; you encourage them, and you listen to their cry, defending the fatherless and the oppressed, in order that man, who is of the earth, may terrify no more.
-Psalm 10:17,18

Day 5

See that you do not look down on one of these little ones. For I tell you that their angels in heaven always see the face of my Father in heaven. -Matthew 18:10

Reflections through the week

_____

_____

_____

_____

_____

_____

_____

_____

_____

_____

Week 4

Unity

Lord, I see so much division in the world and it is easy to observe the trouble caused by that lack of unity. You prayed that Your children would be unified in the truth. May I put down my opinions that are only "my truth" and may I be unified with others on "Your Truth."
Lord, may I be ready to see Your hand at work in my life to teach me "Your Truth." May my life show my peers and my students that I am living that truth well.

Day 1

How good and pleasant it is when brothers live together in unity!
-Psalm 133:1

Day 2

Live in harmony with one another. Do not be proud,
but be willing to associate with people of low position.
Do not be conceited.   -Romans 12:16

Day 3

Let us therefore make every effort to do what leads to peace and
to mutual edification. May the God who gives endurance and
encouragement give you a spirit of unity among yourselves as you
follow Christ Jesus, so that with one heart and mouth you may glorify
the God and Father of our Lord Jesus Christ. -Romans 14:19;15:5,6

Day 4

. . .then make my joy complete by being like-minded, having the same love, being one in spirit and purpose. -Philippians 2:2

Day 5

Finally, all of you, live in harmony with one another; be sympathetic, love as brothers, be compassionate and humble. -1 Peter 3:8

Reflections through the week

_____

_____

_____

_____

_____

_____

_____

_____

_____

_____

Week 5

Creativity

Lord, I look around me and see Your hand. The earth and the sky, the light and the darkness, the rain and the snow, the mighty wind and the gentle breeze all speak to me of Your amazing creativity. Thanks for the reminders of the work that went into creation. What amazes me more is that You created everything from nothing. Thanks for not asking me to do the same. Today, Lord Creator, inspire creativity in me. Sometimes the way that I've always done things clouds my ability to see things from Your perspective. Give to me the sense of how to communicate creatively to my students. Help me to see Your creative work in my own life today.

Day 1

In the beginning God created the heavens and the earth . . . and God saw that it was good. -Genesis 1:1,21

Day 2

Blessed be your glorious name, and may it be exalted above all blessing and praise. You alone are the LORD. You made the heavens, even the highest heavens, and all their starry host, the earth and all that is on it, the seas and all that is in them. You give life to everything, and the multitudes of heaven worship you. -Nehemiah 9:6,7

Day 3

But ask the animals, and they will teach you, or the birds of the air, and they will tell you; or speak to the earth, and it will teach you, or let the fish of the sea inform you. Which of all these does not know

that the hand of the LORD has done this? In his hand is the life
of every creature and the breath of all mankind. -Job 12:7-10

Day 4

Worship him who made the heavens, the earth, the sea,
and the springs of water. -Revelation 14:7b

Day 5

For from Him and through Him and to Him are all things.
To Him be the glory forever! Amen. -Romans 11:3

Reflections through the week

_____

_____

_____

_____

_____

_____

_____

_____

_____

_____

Week 6

Energy

*Lord, what a wonder energy is. Today, I ask for your power
to energize my work. Instead of being drained of energy
today, I am asking that each person, each activity, each
potential problem, each thing that I hear, and each thing that
I say to others will renew my strength and replenish life
energy. May the abundance of Your strength in me fill those
who are empty as I touch lives today.*

Day 1

Now then, just as the LORD promised, he has kept me alive for forty-
five years since the time he said this to Moses, while Israel moved
about in the desert. So here I am today, eighty-five years old! I am still
as strong today as the day Moses sent me out; I'm just as vigorous to go
our to battle now as I was then. Now give me this hill country that the
LORD promised me that day. *-words of Caleb-* Joshua 14:10-11

Day 2

I can do everything through Him who gives me strength.
-Philipians 4:13

Day 3

Therefore we do not lose heart. Though outwardly we are wasting
away, yet inwardly we are being renewed day by day. For our light and
momentary troubles are achieving for us an eternal glory that far
outweighs them all. So we fix our eyes not on what is seen,
but on what is unseen. For what is seen is temporary,
but what is unseen is eternal. -2 Corinthians 4:16-18

Day 4

Even youths grow tired and weary, and young men stumble and fall;
but those who hope in the Lord will renew their strength. They will
soar on wings like eagles; they will run and not grow weary,
they will walk and not be faint. -Isaiah 40:30-31

Day 5

And having put on the new man, which is renewed in
knowledge after the image of him that created him.   -Colossians 3:10

Reflections through the week

_____

_____

_____

_____

_____

_____

_____

_____

_____

_____

Week 7

Focus

Lord, the trivial circumstances of my life seem to scream louder for my attention than the things that I think are most important. While I intend to focus my attention on the people and the tasks that matter most, often I allow the distractions to get me off course. I know that the little details of life are important and must be done, but I pray today that You will help me give my self wholeheartedly to the things that are most important. Help me to see, not simply what is most important to me, but to see what You think is most important for me. While I want to do so much, help me to do a few things well.

Day 1

. . .But one thing I do: Forgetting what is behind and straining toward what is ahead, I press on toward the goal to win the prize for which God has called me heavenward in Christ Jesus. -Philippians 3:13b-14

Day 2

Now devote your heart and soul to seeking the Lord your God.
-1 Chronicles 22:19a

Day 3

Why spend money on what is not bread, and your labor on what does not satisfy? Listen, listen to me, and eat what is good, and your soul will delight in the richest of fare. Give ear and come to me: hear me, that your soul may live.   -Isaiah 55:2-3b

Day 4

Only be careful, and watch yourselves closely
so that you do not forget the things your eyes have seen
or let them slip from your heart as long as you live.
Teach them to your children and to their children after them.

-Deuteronomy 4:9

Day 5

Above all else, guard your heart, for it is the wellspring of life.
-Proverbs 4:23

Reflections through the week

_____

_____

_____

_____

_____

_____

_____

_____

_____

_____

Week 8

Others

Lord, I live in a world that is caught up in self interest. The tendency to be caught up in my own life-challenges is quite often the pattern of my life. Today, dear Lord, I need a balance between my responsibility to bear my own burden and my responsibility to help bear my neighbor's burden. Even though my personal life-projects may not be finished, may I be willing and ready to help someone else in theirs, realizing that You will make a way for me to finish mine. Thanks for teaching me to care for others by doing for me what I cannot do and helping me to do what I can do.

Day 1

Each of you should look not only on your own interests, but also to the interests of others. -Philippians 2:4

Day 2

Do not let any unwholesome talk come out of your mouths, but only what is helpful for building others up according to their needs , that it may benefit those who listen. -Ephesians 4:29

Day 3

Carry each other's burdens, and in this way you will fulfill the law of Christ, if anyone thinks he is something when he is nothing he deceives himself. Each one should test his own actions. Then he can take pride in himself, without comparing himself to somebody else, for each one should carry his own load." -Galatians 6:2-5

Day 4

Be devoted to one another in brotherly love.
Honor one another above yourselves. -Romans 12:10

Day 5

And the things you have heard me say in the presence of
many witnesses entrust to reliable men who will
also be qualified to teach others. -2 Timothy 2:2

Reflections through the week

_____

_____

_____

_____

_____

_____

_____

_____

_____

_____

Week 9

Self-Evaluation

"Search me, O God, and know my heart, try me and see if there be any hurtful way in me and lead me in the everlasting way." Lord, I know that personal honesty is crucial to my understanding of how this life works. As I teach others today may I do so with a clarity about the fact that You . . . know me. The things in my life that You want to change I am willing to change if You will make them clear to me. May the personal honesty that I have with You be evident in my communication today.

Day 1

Test me, O Lord, and try me, examine my heart and my mind.
-Psalm 26:2

Day 2

May the words of my mouth and the meditation of my heart be pleasing in your sight, O Lord, my Rock and my Redeemer. -Psalm 19:14

Day 3

But if we judged ourselves, we would not come under judgement.
-1 Corinthians 11:31

Day 4

Examine yourselves to see whether you are in the faith;
test yourselves. -2 Corinthians 13:5a

Day 5

Search me, O God, and know my heart; test me and know my
anxious thoughts. See if there is any offensive way in me,
and lead me in the way everlasting. -Psalm 139:23, 24

Reflections through the week

_____

_____

_____

_____

_____

_____

_____

_____

_____

_____

Week 10

Time

Lord, I just don't seem to have enough time. The mound of papers that I thought I finished just grew another inch. My life seems pushed out to the edge of the paper and there isn't any margin at the edge. Oh, Lord, right now help me to know that all of this pressure can produce in me again a trust and dependence upon Your strength. You and I both know that I cannot teach effectively alone.

Today, by Your power, I will make the most of each moment You have given me.

Day 1

But when the time had fully come, God sent his Son, born of a woman, born under law, to redeem those under law that we might receive the full rights of sons. -Galatians 4:4,5

Day 2

Be very careful, then, how you live-not as unwise but as wise, making the most of every opportunity, because the days are evil. -Ephesians 5:15,16

Day 3

And he swore by him who lives for ever and ever,
who created the heavens and all that is in them,
the earth and all that is in it, and the sea and all that is in it,
and said, "There will be no more delay!" -Revelation 10:6

Day 4

Therefore keep watch, because you do not know the day or the hour.
-Matthew 25:12

Day 5

But do not forget this one thing, dear friends:
With the Lord a day is like a thousands years,
and a thousand years are like a day. -2 Peter 3:8

Reflections through the week

_____

_____

_____

_____

_____

_____

_____

_____

_____

Week 11

Passion

Lord, You are amazing! My life is full because You have granted me life for this, another day. Today You have entrusted me with young people with passion. Some of their passion is for doing right. Some of their passion is for doing wrong. Today, help me to be passionate about the right things. May my words and actions encourage them to pursue their passion for doing right.

Day 1

Blessed are those who hunger and thirst for righteousness,
for they will be filled. -Matthew 5:6

Day 2

The lions may grow weak and hungry,
but those who seek the LORD lack no good thing. -Psalm 34:10

Day 3

Then you will call upon me and come and pray to me,
and I will listen to you. You will seek me and find me
when you seek me with all your heart. -Jeremiah 29:12,13

Day 4

Trust in the LORD and do good; dwell in the land and enjoy safe
pasture. Delight yourself in the LORD and
He will give you the desires of your heart. -Psalm 37:3,4

Day 5

Blessed are they who keep his statutes and
seek him with all their heart. -Psalm 119:2

Reflections through the week

_____

_____

_____

_____

_____

_____

_____

_____

_____

_____

Week 12

Forgiveness

Lord, thank you for forgiveness. What a powerful, compassionate concept that a person can do wrong against someone but when they truly admit that wrong, the offense can be forgiven by that same person. Lord, Your model prayer says, "Forgive us our sins as we forgive those who sin against us." You have forgiven me much. How can I not give forgiveness to those who I believe have hurt me? May I teach these students today that to forgive is the greatest gift of all.

Day 1

You are forgiving and good, O LORD, abounding in love to all who call to you. Hear my prayer, O LORD; listen to my cry for mercy.
-Psalm 86:5,6

Day 2

Forgive us our debts, as we also have forgiven our debtors.
-Matthew 6:12

Day 3

If your enemy is hungry, give him food to eat; if he is thirsty, give him water to drink. In doing this, you will heap burning coals on his head, and the Lord will reward you. -Proverbs 25:21,22

Day 4

Be kind and compassionate to one another, forgiving each other,
just as in Christ God forgave you. -Ephesians 4:32

Day 5

Do not repay evil with evil or insult with insult, but with blessing,
because to this you were called so that you may inherit a blessing.
-1 Peter 3:9

Reflections through the week

_____

_____

_____

_____

_____

_____

_____

_____

_____

_____

Week 13

Strategy

Lord, I'm always drawing up plans for the next activity or lesson. Thank You for the opportunity to make a plan and then for the energy to carry out that plan. Today, as I work those plans, may I be strategic in my execution of them. Lord, may each activity, each story, each communication with each student have an intended purpose. Help me to keep in mind today my original intentions for that exercise. Help me to cut out the things today that are not complementary to my overall purpose.

Day 1

To man belong the plans of the heart, but from the Lord comes the reply of the tongue. Commit to the Lord whatever you do, and your plans will succeed. -Proverbs 16:1, 3

Day 2

But blessed is the man who trusts in the Lord, whose confidence is in him. He will be like a tree planted by the water that sends out its roots by the stream. -Jeremiah 17:7, 8

Day 3

Let love and faithfulness never leave you; bind them around your neck, write them on the tablet of your heart. Then you will win favor and a good name in the sight of God and man. -Proverbs 3:3,4

Day 4

The integrity of the upright guides them,
but the unfaithful are destroyed by their duplicity.   -Proverbs 11:3

Day 5

Misfortune pursues the sinner, but prosperity is the reward of the
righteous. A good man leaves an inheritance for his children's
children, but a sinner's wealth is stored up for the righteous.
-Proverbs 13:21,22

Reflections through the week

_____

_____

_____

_____

_____

_____

_____

_____

_____

_____

Week 14

Motive

Lord, why am I teaching? Even though my motive seems clear I sometimes doubt how pure those motives really are. Today, I reaffirm to You some of the reasons why I am teaching.

- *I love You.*
- *I love learning.*
- *I love kids.*
- *I love the "light bulb" syndrome (when they really "get it").*
- *I love the work that opens their minds to the world around them.*
- *I love their energy.*
- *I love to teach.*

Thanks again for the opportunity and the tools to teach!

Day 1

All a man's ways seem innocent to him,
but motives are weighed by the Lord. -Proverbs 16:2

Day 2

I the Lord search the heart and examine the mind, to reward a man
according to his conduct, according to what his deeds deserve.
-Jeremiah 17:10

Day 3

So that your giving may be in secret. Then your Father,
who sees what is done in secret, will reward you. -Matthew 6:4

Day 4

He said to them, "You are the ones who justify yourselves in the eyes
of men, but God knows your hearts. What is highly valued among
men is detestable in God's sight." -Luke 16:15

Day 5

Dear children, let us not love with words or tongue but with
actions and in truth. This then is how we know that we belong to the
truth, and how we set our hearts at rest in his presence whenever our
hearts condemn us. For God is greater than our hearts,
and He knows everything. -1 John 3:20

Reflections through the week

Week 15

Questions

Lord, You, the greatest Teacher, ask great questions—questions where the answer is already known by You. I am reminded of Your questions, "Where are you?" "What is that in your hand?" "What do you want me to do for you?" The power and the pointed purpose of Your questions make plainYour passion to lead me toward the discovery of truth. Your questions leave room for my own heart to search and find the answer. Today, help me to remember the discovery potential of a well-asked question! May the questions that I ask excite and illuminate the truths I desire to teach.

Day 1

But the LORD God called to the man,
"Where are you?"
-Genesis 3:9

Day 2

Then the Lord said to Cain,
"Where is your brother Abel?"
-Genesis 4:9

Day 3

Then the Lord said to him [Moses],
"What is that in your hand?"
-Exodus 4:2

Day 4

After three days they found him [Jesus] in the temple courts,
sitting among the teachers, listening to them and
asking them questions. -Luke 2:46

Day 5

Jesus straightened up and asked her, "Woman, where are they?
Has no one condemned you?" "No one, sir," she said.
Then neither do I condemn you," Jesus declared.
"Go now and leave your life of sin."   -John 8:10,11

Reflections through the week

_____

_____

_____

_____

_____

_____

_____

_____

_____

_____

Week 16

Failure

Lord, there are some areas in my life where I'm just not doing well. In fact, I'm failing. Instead of becoming discouraged by failure, help me to remember that failure teaches me what doesn't work. In the wake of my failure, lead me to what does work. Today, may the seed of failure die so that it can germinate and become the flower of success. Thank you for allowing me to fail today's progress report. My grade card helps me to remember that I can continue to change and grow. Help me to convey the same "fruit from failure" attitude to my students today.

Day 1
I tell the truth, unless a kernel of wheat falls to the ground and dies, it remains only a single seed. But if it dies, it produces many seeds.
-John 12:24

Day 2
So I find this law at work: When I want to do good, evil is right there with me. What a wretched man I am! Who will rescue me from this body of death? Thanks be to God-through Jesus Christ our Lord! Therefore, there is now no condemnation for those who are in Christ Jesus. -Romans 7:21, 24, 25; 8:1

Day 3
My life is consumed by anguish and my years by groaning; my strength fails because of my affliction, and my bones grow weak. But I trust in you, O Lord; I say, "You are my God." My times are in your hands; deliver my from my enemies. -Psalm 31:10, 14,15

Day 4

"Now I am about to go the way of all the earth. You know with all your heart and soul that not one of all the good promises the Lord your God gave you has failed. Every promise has been fulfilled; not one has failed." -Joshua 23:14

Day 5

My flesh and my heart may fail, but God is the strength of my heart and my portion forever. -Psalm 73:26

Reflections through the week

_____

_____

_____

_____

_____

_____

_____

_____

_____

_____

_____

_____

Week 17

Hurt

Lord, my heart is broken when I look into the eyes of my students and see their hurt. Much of the hurt I see is caused by insensitivity, selfishness or the cruelty of others. Lord, I know that You feel, understand and want to fix their hurts by helping them to learn from them. Today, Lord, may I have the sensitivity and the wisdom to see those who need an encouraging word. May I demonstrate Your empathy and communicate compassion in the midst of their pain.

Day 1

When Jesus landed and saw a large crowd, he had compassion on them, because they were like sheep without a shepherd. So he began teaching them many things. -Mark 6:34

Day 2

When the Lord saw her, his heart went out to her and he said, "Don't cry." -Luke 7:13

Day 3

For you know the grace of our Lord Jesus Christ, that though he was rich, yet for your sakes he became poor, so that you through his poverty might become rich. -2 Corinthians 8:9

Day 4

For we do not have a high priest who is unable to sympathize with our
weaknesses, but we have one who has been tempted in every way,
just as we are-yet without sin. -Hebrews 4:15

Day 5

For I was hungry and you gave me something to eat, I was thirsty and
you gave me something to drink, I was a stranger and you invited me
in, I needed clothes and you clothed me, I was sick and you looked
after me, I was in prison and you came to visit me. Then the righteous
will answer him, 'Lord, when did we see you hungry and feed you, or
thirsty and give you something to drink? When did we see you a
stranger and invite you in, or needing clothes and clothe you? When
did we see you sick or in prison and go to visit you?' "The King will
reply, 'I tell you the truth, whatever you did for one of the least of
these brothers of mind, you did for me." -Matthew 25:35-40

Reflections through the week

_____

_____

_____

_____

_____

_____

_____

_____

_____

_____

Week 18

Yes

*Lord, "yes," is a wonderful word that affirms to me the
potential that Your love has placed within me. So many
aspects of my life necessitate a "no" or "wait." "Yes" says
"Go; I can; try." "Yes" is an attitude that reflects the thinking of the heart about all the possibilities. Life often seems
bound by "no" but is liberated by "yes." Both are important
bookends for a balanced life; but if I'm going to be out of
balance, help me to tip towards the "yes" end of the scale.
May the lives I touch today hear the excitement and grace of
"yes" in my voice.*

Day 1

For no matter how many promises God has made, they are "Yes"
in Christ. And so through him the "Amen" is spoken
by us to the glory of God. -2 Corinthians 1:20

Day 2

"Do you hear what these children are saying?" They asked him, "Yes,"
replied Jesus, "have you never read, " ' From the lips of children and
infants you have ordained praise'? " -Matthew 21:16

Day 3

Above all, my brothers, do not swear-not by heaven or by earth or by
anything else. Let your "Yes" be yes, and your "No," no,
or you will be condemned. -James 5:12

Day 4

Yes, the Lord will give what is good,
and our land will yield its increase. -Psalm 85:12 (Amplified)

Day 5

Then I heard a voice from heaven, say, "Write: Blessed are the dead
who die in the Lord from now on." "Yes," says the Spirit, "they will
rest from their labor, for their deeds will follow them."
-Revelation 14:12

Reflections through the week

_____

_____

_____

_____

_____

_____

_____

_____

_____

_____

_____

Week 19

No

*Lord, "no" is a boundary word. It is one of the ways that You
protect me from danger. You know that You have given me
some students who need the protection of more clearly defined
boundaries. The impact of "no" in my life as well as in theirs
is for safety and discipline. To say "no" in some situations is
necessary and easy while in some others "no" is hard to say
and even harder to follow through. Lord, help me to think
through each request today and choose my "no's" carefully.*

Day 1

"You shall have no other gods before me." -Exodus 20:3

Day 2

"No one can serve two masters. Either he will hate the one and love
the other, or he will be devoted to the one and despise the other. You
cannot serve both God and Money." -Matthew 6:24

Day 3

He [Jesus] said to his disciples, "Why are you so afraid?
Do you still have no faith?" -Mark 4:40

Day 4

And she gave birth to her firstborn, a son.
She wrapped him in cloths and placed him in a manger,
because there was no room for them in the inn. -Luke 2:7

Day 5

No, in all these things we are more than conquerors
through him who loved us. -Romans 8:37

Reflections through the week

_____

_____

_____

_____

_____

_____

_____

_____

_____

_____

Week 20

Fog

Lord, sometimes school is delayed by a thick layer of fog in the early morning. Visibility is difficult and consequently moving forward anywhere is often dangerous and sometimes impossible. Today, help me be the one who brings the clarity of the sun to burn away the fog for my students. Some have fog from home, some from society, all have fog from inside themselves. May the fog be burned away as I clearly communicate the concepts of truth.

Day 1
When Jesus spoke again to the people, he said, "I am the light of the world. Whoever follows me will never walk in darkness, but will have the light of life." -John 8:12

Day 2
I will lead the blind by ways they have not known, along unfamiliar paths I will guide them; I will turn the darkness into light before them and make the rough places smooth. These are the things I will do; I will not forsake them. -Isaiah 42:16

Day 3
For the Lord God is a sun and shield; the Lord bestows favor and honor; no good thing does he withhold from those whose walk is blameless. -Psalm 84:11

Day 4

But may they who love you be like the sun when it rises in its strength.
-Judges 5:31b

Day 5

Whoever loves his brother lives in the light, and there is nothing in
him to make him stumble. -1 John 2:10

Reflections through the week

_____

_____

_____

_____

_____

_____

_____

_____

_____

_____

Week 21

Foundations

Lord, You made me a builder. I am laying one brick of knowledge at a time to shape a life. The bricks are the same, but they come together uniquely because each life-structure is different. Today, help me to know what knowledge is needed for each of my students. May I place each brick with care and be patient enough to allow the mortar to dry so that each life may stand the test of time.

Day 1

Therefore everyone who hears these words of mine and puts them into practice is like a wise man who built his house on the rock. The rain came down, the streams rose, and the winds blew and beat against that house; yet it did not fall, because it had its foundation on the rock. But everyone who hears these words of mine and does not put them into practice is like a foolish man who built his house on sand. The rain came down, the streams rose, and the winds blew and beat against that house, and it fell with a great crash. -Matthew 7:24-27

Day 2

By the grace God has given me, I laid a foundation as an expert builder, and someone else is building on it. But each one should be careful how he builds. For no one can lay any foundation other than the one already laid, which is Jesus Christ. -1 Corinthians 3:10, 11

Day 3

So this is what the Sovereign LORD says: "See, I lay a stone in Zion, a tested stone, a precious cornerstone for a sure foundation; the one who trusts will never be dismayed." -Isaiah 28:16

Day 4

Now we know that if the earthly tent we live in is destroyed, we have
a building from God, an eternal house in heaven,
not built by human hands. -2 Corinthians 5:1

Day 5

Nevertheless, God's foundation stands firm,
sealed with this inscription:
"The Lord knows those who are his," and, "Everyone who confesses
the name of the Lord must turn away from wickedness."
-2 Timothy 2:19

Reflections through the week

Week 22

Wisdom

Lord, it is the day-to-day "stuff" of my life that shows me I need Your wisdom. The wisdom is needed not so much because the decisions I make are so monumental, but because I simply need Your perspective on people and events. Your Word reminds me to ask for wisdom if I need it. Lord, I need Your wisdom and I ask for Your wisdom, today. May my heart be ready to receive Your wisdom and may I clearly see today the people and events that You use to deliver that wisdom. Thank You for the dynamic truths of Your Word that continue to point me to You and Your ways.

Day 1
He made the earth by his power; he founded the world by his wisdom and stretched out the heavens by his understanding. -Jeremiah 51:15

Day 2
For the foolishness of God is wiser than man's wisdom, and the weakness of God is stronger than man's strength. -1 Corinthians 1:25

Day 3
This is what the Lord says: "Let not the wise man boast of his wisdom or the strong man boast of his strength or the rich man boast of his riches, but let him who boasts boast about this: that he understands and knows me, that I am the Lord, who exercises kindness, justice and righteousness on earth, for in these I delight," declares the Lord.
-Jeremiah 9:23,24

Day 4

How much better to get wisdom than gold, to choose understanding rather than silver! Whoever gives heed to instruction prospers, and blessed is he who trusts in the Lord. -Proverbs 16:16,20

Day 5

If any of you lacks wisdom, he should ask God, who gives generously to all without finding fault, and it will be given to him. -James 1:5

Reflections through the week

_____

_____

_____

_____

_____

_____

_____

_____

_____

_____

Week 23

Purpose

Lord, remind me again why I am a teacher. Does what I say really sink in? Am I making an impact on those who have so little support? Do I communicate in a way that will help these kids to really change? Help me to remember that You, the greatest Teacher, faithfully taught even though You knew that some would not understand. Today, may my purpose be rekindled with the life-changing thought that my main purpose is to be pleasing to You.

Day 1
So we make it our goal to please him, whether we are at home in the body or away from it. For we must all appear before the judgment seat of Christ, that each one may receive what is due him for the things done while in the body, whether good or bad. -2 Corinthians 5:9, 10

Day 2
As long as it is day, we must do the work of him who sent me. Night is coming, when no one can work. -John 9:4

Day 3
So whether you eat or drink or whatever you do, do it all for the glory of God. -1 Corinthians 10:31

Day 4

Whatever you do, work at it with all your heart, as working for the Lord, not for men, since you know that you will receive an inheritance from the Lord as a reward. It is the Lord Christ you are serving.
-Colossians 3:23, 24

Day 5

Great are your purposes and mighty are your deeds. Your eyes are open to all the ways of men; you reward everyone according to his conduct and as his deeds deserve. -Jeremiah 32:19

Reflections through the week

_____

_____

_____

_____

_____

_____

_____

_____

_____

_____

Week 24

Winning

Lord, my students love to win. They always work harder at the learning activities when we play some kind of competitive game. Most of them have some sports team they cheer for or some sport they love. The concept of winning is part of real life. Today, help me to use that winning desire to motivate the competitors to find a way to win at learning the character skills of life. For the students who are not captivated by the winning concept—may I find the motivating force for them as well.

Day 1

Do you not know that in a race all the runners run, but only one gets the prize? Run in such a way as to get the prize. Everyone who competes in the games goes into strict training. They do it to get a crown that will not last; but we do it to get a crown that will last forever.
-1 Corinthians 9:24,25

Day 2

I have fought the good fight, I have finished the race,
I have kept the faith. -2 Timothy 4:7

Day 3

I press on toward the goal to win the prize for which God has called me heavenward in Christ Jesus. -Philippians 3:14

Day 4

Therefore, since we are surrounded by such a great cloud of witnesses, let us throw off everything that hinders and the sin that so easily entangles, and let us run with perseverance the race marked out for us.
-Hebrews 12:1

Day 5

However, I consider my life worth nothing to me, if only I may finish the race and complete the task the Lord Jesus has given me-the task of testifying to the gospel of God's grace. -Acts 20:24

Reflections through the week

_____

_____

_____

_____

_____

_____

_____

_____

_____

_____

Week 25

Losing

Lord, in the world where I live, losing is not accepted well. It seems that everybody wants to win at all costs. In the sporting world each year only one is crowned "the winner." Losing is what helps to really show the heart attitudes of the participant. Help me to remember and teach that more lessons can be learned through losing then through winning. Today, as my students learn the pain of losing, help me to encourage them to handle defeat with grace. May it motivate them to help others who are struggling with losing.

Day 1

Whoever finds his life will lose it, and whoever loses his life
for my sake will find it. -Matthew 10:39

Day 2

For whoever wants to save his life will lose it, but whoever loses his
life for me will find it. What good will it be for a man if he gains the
whole world, yet forfeits his soul? Or what can a man give
in exchange for his soul? -Matthew 16:25, 26

Day 3

Rejoice with those who rejoice,
and weep with those who weep.
-Romans 12:15

Day 4

Blessed be the God and Father of our Lord Jesus Christ, the Father of mercies and God of all comfort, who comforts us in all our affliction so that we will be able to comfort those who are in any affliction with the comfort with which we ourselves are comforted by God.

-2 Corinthians 1:3-4

Day 5

Consider him [Jesus] who endured such opposition from sinful men, so that you will not grow weary and lose heart. -Hebrews 12:3

Reflections through the week

_____

_____

_____

_____

_____

_____

_____

_____

_____

_____

Week 26

Strength

Lord, often I begin each day tired and I end it exhausted. I need Your strength. May I not depend on my strength, but remember each moment that I can do all things I need to do through You. May my mind control my body today so that even though I may feel weak, I will be strengthened mentally, physically and spiritually as I live in Your strength. Today, help me to make wise decisions about what I put into my mind and also the foods that I put into my body. May I model for my students what it means to have a Godly balance in life.

Day 1

Finally, be strong in the Lord and in his mighty power.
-Ephesians 6:10

Day 2

Observe therefore all the commands I am giving you today, so that you may have the strength to go in and take over the land that you are crossing the Jordan to possess. -Deuteronomy 11:8

Day 3

Be strong and courageous. Do not be afraid or terrified because of them, for the Lord your God goes with you;
He will never leave you nor forsake you. -Deuteronomy 31:6

Day 4

. . .Love the Lord you God with all your heart and with all your soul and with all your strength and with all your mind. . . -Luke 10:27

Day 5

But he said to me, "My grace is sufficient for you, for my power is made perfect in weakness." Therefore I will boast all the more gladly about my weaknesses, so that Christ's power may rest on me.
-2 Corinthians 12:9

Reflections through the week

_____

_____

_____

_____

_____

_____

_____

_____

_____

_____

Week 27

Keys

Lord, I often hear the idea that there are "seven keys for this," or the "key to that is...." The well intentioned desire is to help simplify the lives of people. The more complex our technological advances make our world, the more we cry out for simplicity in life. I need some keys to open the doors that fit my life, but I'm not sure I have yet found them. I know there are at least two keys that have been clearly defined for me already—the Word of God and my active obedient response to its truth. Today, help me use the keys I know I have and teach my students that these are the sure keys for life.

Day 1

The grass withers and the flowers fall, but the Word of our God stands forever. -Isaiah 40:8

Day 2

And now these three remain: faith , hope and love.
But the greatest of these is love.
-1 Corinthians 13:13

Day 3

But the fruit of the Spirit is love, joy, peace, patience, kindness, goodness, faithfulness, gentleness and self-control. -Galatians 5:22,23

Day 4

Trust in the Lord with all your heart and lean not on your own
understanding; in all your ways acknowledge him,
and he will make your paths straight. -Proverbs 3:5, 6

Day 5

Jesus answered, "I am the way and the truth and the life. No one comes
to the Father except through me." -John 14:6

Reflections through the week

_____

_____

_____

_____

_____

_____

_____

_____

_____

_____

Week 28

Growth

*Lord, to grow is to purposefully change in the right direction.
Every day when I look out the window, I see Your pattern of
growth in action. My students are physically growing every
day, help me to teach them to spiritually grow. Lord, You
have given me the privilege to see their skills increase. Their
ability to think and reason is better now than when they came
to me. Some of their growth is born of their growing age,
some of experience, some of study. Some, I hope, has been
facilitated by me, their model for growth. Today, O Lord,
may I model in my listening, speaking, and thinking a
willingness to follow Jesus and a readiness to really grow.*

Day 1

And Jesus grew in wisdom and stature,
and in favor with God and men. -Luke 2:52

Day 2

And the boy Samuel continued to grow in stature
and in favor with the Lord and with men. -1 Samuel 2:26

Day 3

My son, do not forget my teaching, but keep my commands in your
heart, for they will prolong your life many years and bring you prosperity. Let love and faithfulness never leave you: bind them around your
neck, write them on the tablet of you heart. Then you will win favor
and a good name in the sight of God and man. -Proverbs 3:1-4

Day 4

The fear of the Lord is the beginning of wisdom, and knowledge of the
holy One is understanding. For through me your days will be many,
and years will be added to your life. The fear of the Lord adds length
to life, but the years of the wicked are cut short.
-Proverbs 9:10,11; 10:27

Day 5

Like newborn babies, crave pure spiritual milk, so that by it you may
grow up in your salvation. -1 Peter 2:2

Reflections through the week

_____

_____

_____

_____

_____

_____

_____

_____

_____

_____

Week 29

Faith

*Lord, to see without my eyes, to hear without my ears, to feel
without my hands, to smell without my nose, to taste without
my tongue must be a picture of what it means to live by faith.
My tendency is to trust me, what I can see, hear, feel, smell,
and taste. Faith, Lord, teaches me to live according to what
You say. It is not that my faith cannot benefit from my senses;
it is that my senses often do not want to live by my faith.
Today, may my faith in You lead in every area of
my life.*

Day 1
But let all who take refuge in you be glad; let them ever sing for joy.
Spread your protection over them, that those
who love your name may rejoice in you. -Psalm 5:11

Day 2
You will keep in perfect peace him whose mind is steadfast, because he
trusts in you. Trust in the Lord forever, for the Lord,
the Lord, is the Rock eternal. -Isaiah 26:3,4

Day 3
Fear of man will prove to be a snare, but whoever trusts in the Lord is
kept safe. -Proverbs 29:25

Day 4

. . . .so that your faith might not rest on men's wisdom,
but on God's power. -1 Corinthians 2:5

Day 5

And without faith it is impossible to please God, because anyone who
comes to him must believe that he exists and
that he rewards those who earnestly seek him. -Hebrews 11:6

Reflections through the week

Week 30

Future

Lord, keeping my heart fixed on the future while living out the details of today is a tough assignment. What is yet to come during this school year is quickly approaching and yet each day is filled with tasks that need to be accomplished, lessons that must be completed and students who must be motivated to maximize today's opportunities. Help me to see the way in which each task today will lead to the fulfillment of tomorrow. May my thinking be rooted in the present but reaching upward to the future.

Day 1

Therefore we do not lose heart. Though outwardly we are wasting away, yet inwardly we are being renewed day by day. For our light and momentary troubles are achieving for us an eternal glory that far outweighs them all. So we fix our eyes not on what is seen, but on what is unseen. For what is seen is temporary, but what is unseen is eternal. -2 Corinthians 4:16-18

Day 2

And the God of all grace, who called you to his eternal glory in Christ, after you have suffered a little while, will himself restore you and make you strong, firm and steadfast. To him be the power forever and ever. Amen. -1 Peter 5:10-11

Day 3

Fight the good fight of the faith. Take hold of the eternal life to which you were called when you made your good confession in the presence of many witnesses. -1 Timothy 6:12

Day 4

Now this is eternal life: that they may know you, the only true God,
and Jesus Christ, whom you have sent. -John 17:3

Day 5

Simon Peter answered him, "Lord to whom shall we go?
You have the words of eternal life." -John 6:68

Reflections through the week

_____

_____

_____

_____

_____

_____

_____

_____

_____

_____

Week 31

Recess

---

*Lord, even though You didn't need it, on the seventh day You
taught us that we need an occasional break. Recess is one of
those occasional breaks. Recess is all about a change in
scenery—a wonderful opportunity to run, jump, yell, chase,
swing, enjoy the laughter of friends and just play. Today,
help me to find time for recess somewhere in the midst of the
circumstances of my life. May the beauty of a God-provided
recess give me rest from the challenges of my teaching.*

Day 1

By the seventh day God had finished the work he had been doing;
so on the seventh day he rested from all his work. -Genesis 2:2

Day 2

So whether you eat or drink or whatever you do,
do it all for the glory of God. -1 Corinthians 10:31

Day 3

To the pure all things are pure... -Titus 1:15

Day 4

Every good and perfect gift is from above, coming down from the
Father of the heavenly lights, who does not change
like shifting shadows. -James 1:17

Day 5

. . . and on the fourteenth they rested and
made it a day of feasting and joy. -Esther 9:17

Reflections through the week

_____

_____

_____

_____

_____

_____

_____

_____

_____

_____

Week 32

Parents

Lord, thank You for letting me come alongside to help parents by teaching their children. How you come alongside to teach me, reminds me of Your perfect parenting. I've never seen a perfect set of parents, but I thank You for the ones who take their responsibility seriously and who want Your best for their kids. May the things I say and do help each family. Today, help me to see in the lives of my students what their parents are doing right. May my words support what good things they seek to accomplish in the lives of their children.

Day 1

If anyone does not provide for his relatives,
and especially for his immediate family,
he has denied the faith and
is worse than an unbeliever. -1 Timothy 5:8

Day 2

Train a child in the way he should go,
and when he is old he will not turn from it. -Proverbs 22:6

Day 3

Fathers, do not embitter your children,
or they will become discouraged. -Colossians 3:21
Fathers, do not exasperate your children; instead, bring them up
in the training and instruction of the Lord. -Ephesians 6:4

Day 4

My son, do not despise the Lord's discipline and do not resent his
rebuke, because the Lord disciplines those he loves,
as a father the son he delights in. -Proverbs 3:12

Day 5

Only be careful, and watch yourselves closely so that you do not forget
the things your eyes have seen or let them slip from your heart as long
as you live. Teach them to your children and to
their children after them. -Deuteronomy 4:9

Reflections through the week

_____

_____

_____

_____

_____

_____

_____

_____

_____

_____

_____

Week 33

Weakness

Lord, my weaknesses are ever before me although sometimes they are hard to admit. One of my occupational hazards is the necessity to always "be together." That hazard makes it especially difficult to admit my weakness. In my weakness, I need your strength . Lord, today I humbly admit my weakness and I ask for your strength. I will actively rest in the strength that only You provide for people who know their weakness.

Day 1

But he said to me, "My grace is sufficient for you, for my power is made perfect in weakness." Therefore I will boast all the more gladly about my weaknesses, so that Christ's power may rest on me.
-2 Corinthians 12:10

Day 2

For the foolishness of God is wiser than man's wisdom,
and the weakness of God is stronger that man's strength.
-1 Corinthians 1:25

Day 3

For to be sure, he was crucified in weakness, yet he lives by God's
power. Likewise, we are weak in him, yet by God's power
we will live with him to serve you. -2 Corinthians 13:4

Day 4

Who through faith conquered kingdoms, administered justice, and
gained what was promised; who shut the mouths of lions, quenched
the fury of the flames, and escaped the edge of the sword;
whose weakness was turned to strength. . . -Hebrews 11:33,34

Day 5

Not that we are competent in ourselves to claim anything for
ourselves, but our competence comes from God. -2 Corinthians 3:5

Reflections through the week

_____

_____

_____

_____

_____

_____

_____

_____

_____

_____

Week 34

Consistency

Lord, I heard somewhere that 90% of life is simply "showing up." My students "show up" consistently but there is so much more in their lives that could occur if that consistency were focused on the right things. My consistency is only as good as the direction that it is headed. Today, I want to be consistently moving toward a goal and demonstrating the evidence of Your work in me. The consitency that You model is what I want visible in my life. As my students watch my life may I display a well-directed consistency.

Day 1

Whoever can be trusted with very little can also be trusted with much, and whoever is dishonest with very little will also be dishonest with much. So if you have not been trustworthy in handling worldly wealth, who will trust you with true riches? And if you have not been trustworthy with someone else's property, who will give your property of your own? -Luke 16:10-12

Day 2

Love the Lord, all his saints! The Lord preserves the faithful, but the proud he pays back in full. -Psalm 31:23

Day 3

A faithful man will be richly blessed. . . -Proverbs 28:20

Day 4

Whatever you do, work at it with all your heart, as working for the Lord, not for men, since you know that you will receive an inheritance from the Lord as a reward. It is the Lord Christ you are serving.
-Colossians 3:22

Day 5

Now it is required that those who have been given a trust must prove faithful. -1 Corinthians 4:2

Reflections through the week

_____

_____

_____

_____

_____

_____

_____

_____

_____

_____

_____

Week 35

Loving

Lord, I am the product of your love. You taught me that love sacrifices for another's ultimate good. I am thankful for others today who love me. Some know little about me, but they love me. Some know a lot about me and they love me. You know all about me, and You still love me. Thank you! Today, may my students experience the love that I have received from You. May it motivate them to love others as You have loved me.

Day 1
Love the LORD your God with all your heart and
with all your soul and with all your strength. -Deuteronomy 6:5

Day 2
But be very careful to keep the commandment and the law that Moses
the servant of the LORD gave you: to love the LORD your God, to
walk in all his ways, to obey his commands, to hold fast to him and
to serve him with all your heart and all your soul.
-Deuteronomy 2:4

Day 3
Instead, speaking the truth in love, we will in all things grow up into
him who is the head, that is, Christ. -Ephesians 4:15

Day 4

I pray that out of his glorious riches he may strengthen you with power through his Spirit in Your inner being, so that Christ may dwell in your hearts through faith. And I pray that you, being rooted and established in love, may have power, together with all the saints, to grasp how wide and long and high and deep is the love of Christ, and to know this love that surpasses knowledge-that you may be filled to the measure of all the fullness of God. -Ephesians 3:16

Day 5

God is not unjust; he will not forget your work and the love you have shown him as you have helped his people and continue to help them. -Hebrews 6:10

Reflections through the week

_____

_____

_____

_____

_____

_____

_____

_____

_____

Week 36

Kindness

Lord, a cup of cold water, a touch, a look, a smile, a pat on the back, a kind word, a note—these are expressions of kindness. Some of my students experience very little kindness. At times, others tear down, humiliate, belittle, demean, and demoralize them. Kindness is the hand to help, the ear to hear, the eyes to see, the sacrifice of self for someone else's good. Today, help me to see ways to be kind. As my students think of me, may they think of a kind person.

Day 1

He who despises his neighbor sins,
but blessed is he who is kind to the needy. -Proverbs 14:21

Day 2

Blessed are the merciful, for they will be shown mercy.
Give to the one who asks you, and do not turn away from
the one who wants to borrow from you. -Matthew 5:7,42

Day 3

For I was hungry and you gave me something to eat, I was thirsty and
you gave me something to drink, I was a stranger and you invited me
in, I needed clothes and you clothed me, I was sick and you looked
after me, I was in prison and you came to visit me. I tell you the truth,
whatever you did for one of the least of these brothers of mine,
you did it for me. -Matthew 25:35,36,40

Day 4

In everything I did, I showed you that by this kind of hard work we must help the weak, remembering the words the Lord Jesus himself said: "It is more blessed to give than to receive." -Acts 20:35

Day 5

But love your enemies, do good to them, and lend to them without expecting to get anything back. Then your reward will be great, and you will be sons of the Most High, because he is kind to the ungrateful and wicked. Be merciful, just as your Father is merciful. -Luke 6:35,36

Reflections through the week

_____

_____

_____

_____

_____

_____

_____

_____

_____

_____

Week 37

Flying

Lord, as the mother bird prepares her chicks for flight so I have sought to help my students this year strengthen their wings to fly. To watch them try, falter and fail is a painful but necessary part of the process. Today, may the knowledge, truth, and character that I have endeavored to instill in each student be the wind that You use, O Lord, to help each student soar. I ask that each one might give glory to You for Your work in them.

Day 1

He gives strength to the weary and increases the power of the weak. Even youths grow tired and weary, and young men stumble and fall; but those who hope in the LORD will renew their strength. They will soar on wings like eagles; they will run and not grow weary, they will walk and not be faint.   -Isaiah 40:29-31

Day 2

In a desert land he found him, in a barren and howling waste. He shielded him and cared for him; he guarded him as the apple of his eye, like an eagle that stirs up its nest and hovers over its young, that spreads its wings to catch them and carries them on its pinions.
-Deuteronomy 32:10,11

Day 3

Praise the LORD, O my soul, and forget not all his benefits—who forgives all your sins and heals all your diseases, who redeems your life from the pit and crowns you with love and compassion, who satisfies your desires with good things so that your youth is renewed like the eagle's.   -Psalm 103:2-5

Day 4

If I go up to the heavens, you are there;
if I make my bed in the depths, you are there.
If I rise on the wings of the dawn,
if I settle on the far side of the sea
even there your hand will guide me,
your right hand will hold me fast. -Psalm 139:8-10

Day 5

You yourselves have seen what I did to Egypt, and how
I carried you on eagles' wings and brought you to myself.
-Exodus 19:4

Reflections through the week

_____

_____

_____

_____

_____

_____

_____

_____

_____

_____

Week 38

Examinations

Lord, The word "examination" strikes fear in the hearts of some students while others seem absolutely unaffected by the thought. Exams can not only help my students see how much they have learned but also help them realize how much there is still to learn. I want them to use exams as an opportunity to grow and be honest with themselves about where they really are in life. Today, as I give exams, may my students find the exams useful. Help me in my own life to learn from the exams that You are giving me.

Day 1
For in the same way you judge others, you will be judged, and with the measure you use, it will be measured to you. "Why do you look at the speck of sawdust in your brother's eye and pay no attention to the plank in your own eye? How can you say to your brother, 'Let me take the speck out of your eye,' when all the time there is a plank in your own eye? You hypocrite, first take the plank out of your own eye, and then you will see clearly to remove the speck from your brother's eye. -Matthew 7:2-5

Day 2
Search me, O God, and know my heart; test me and know my anxious thoughts. See if there is any offensive way in me, and lead me in the way everlasting. -Psalm 139:23,24

Day 3
Who can speak and have it happen if the Lord has not decreed it? Is it not from the mouth of the Most High that both calamities and good things come? Why should any living man complain when punished for his sins? Let us examine our ways and test them, and let us return to the LORD. -Lamentations 3:37-40

Day 4

Examine yourselves to see whether you are in the faith; test yourselves. Do you not realize that Christ Jesus is in you—unless, of course, you fail the test? -2 Corinthians 13:5

Day 5

A man ought to examine himself before he eats of the bread and drinks of the cup. For anyone who eats and drinks without recognizing the body of the Lord eats and drinks judgment on himself. That is why many among you are weak and sick, and a number of you have fallen asleep. But if we judged ourselves, we would not come under judgment. When we are judged by the Lord, we are being disciplined so that we will not be condemned with the world.
-1 Corinthians 11:28-32

Reflections through the week

_____

_____

_____

_____

_____

_____

_____

_____

_____

Week 39

Records

Lord, faithfully day after day this year I kept a record of each student's progress. Each student's record has enabled me to focus my teaching on specific areas of learning that need to be developed. Today, Lord, may the idea that we each are leaving a record help to motivate my students to diligent study. Help me to emphasize to my students the imperative of living in such a way that their records show their true progress.

Day 1

So we make it our goal to please him, whether we are at home in the body or away from it. For we must all appear before the judgment seat of Christ, that each one may receive what is due him for the things done while in the body, whether good or bad. -2 Corinthians 5:9,10

Day 2

For no one can lay any foundation other than the one already laid, which is Jesus Christ. If any man builds on this foundation using gold, silver, costly stones, wood, hay or straw, his work will be shown for what it is, because the Day will bring it to light. It will be revealed with fire, and the fire will test the quality of each man's work. If what he has built survives, he will receive his reward. If it is burned up, he will suffer loss; he himself will be saved, but only as one escaping through the flames. -1 Corinthians 3:11-15

Day 3

Let him who does wrong continue to do wrong; let him who is vile continue to be vile; let him who does right continue to do right; and let him who is holy continue to be holy. "Behold, I am coming soon! My reward is with me, and I will give to everyone according to what he has done. I am the Alpha and the Omega, the First and the Last, the Beginning and the End." -Rev. 22:11-13

Day 4

Anyone who does not believe God has made him out to be a liar, because he has not believed the testimony God has given about his Son. And this is the testimony: God has given us eternal life, and this life is in his Son. He who has the Son has life; he who does not have the Son of God does not have life. I write these things to you who believe in the name of the Son of God so that you may know that you have eternal life. -1 John 5:10-13

Day 5

But love your enemies, do good to them, and lend to them without expecting to get anything back. Then your reward will be great, and you will be sons of the Most High, because he is kind to the ungrateful and wicked. Be merciful, just as your Father is merciful. "Do not judge, and you will not be judged. Do not condemn, and you will not be condemned. Forgive, and you will be forgiven. Give, and it will be given to you. A good measure, pressed down, shaken together and running over, will be poured into your lap." -Luke 6:35-38

Reflections through the week

_____

_____

_____

_____

_____

_____

_____

_____

_____

Week 40

Evaluation

Lord, to take the events, circumstances, people, projects, tests and all the other "stuff" that has made up this year and evaluate its purpose, plan and design for my life is beyond my capabilities. To evaluate life is the ability to gain real understanding by learning from any life experience. As I evaluate life in light of Your expectations, may I truly grasp the "value" in what and whom You have allowed me to encounter. Today, may my students see that I am resting in the belief that trusting You, O Lord, creates value out of those experiences and circumstances which seem like they have no value.

Day 1

Consider it pure joy, my brothers, whenever you face trials of many kinds, because you know that the testing of your faith develops perseverance. Perseverance must finish its work so that you may be mature and complete, not lacking anything. If any of you lacks wisdom, he should ask God, who gives generously to all without finding fault, and it will be given to him. -James 1:2-5

Day 2

But Joseph said to them, "Don't be afraid. Am I in the place of God? You intended to harm me, but God intended it for good to accomplish what is now being done, the saving of many lives. So then, don't be afraid. I will provide for you and your children."
And he reassured them and spoke kindly to them. -Genesis 50:19-21

Day 3

Therefore, I urge you, brothers, in view of God's mercy, to offer your bodies as living sacrifices, holy and pleasing to God—this is your spiritual act of worship. Do not conform any longer to the pattern of this world, but be transformed by the renewing of your mind. Then you will be able to test and approve what God's will is--his good, pleasing and perfect will. -Romans 12:1,2

Day 4

Let us not become weary in doing good, for at the proper time we will reap a harvest if we do not give up. Therefore, as we have opportunity, let us do good to all people, especially to those who belong to the family of believers.
-Galatians 6:9,10

Day 5

Now, O LORD my God, you have made your servant king in place of my father David. But I am only a little child and do not know how to carry out my duties. . . So give your servant a discerning heart to govern your people and to distinguish between right and wrong. For who is able to govern this great people of yours?" The Lord was pleased that Solomon had asked for this.
-1 Kings 3:7-10

Reflections through the week

_____

_____

_____

_____

_____

_____

_____

_____

_____

_____

Week 41

Commendation

Lord, My students love to hear their name called and to be praised for a job well done. My remarks on their papers mean much more to them than I realize. Of course I know how they feel because I love that same satisfaction when I hear that my work is noticed and appreciated. Today, may my life be worthy of receiving a commendation of praise from You. As I interact with the people You have entrusted to me, help me to notice their contribution and commend them.

Day 1

I was glad when Stephanas, Fortunatus and Achaicus arrived, because they have supplied what was lacking from you. For they refreshed my spirit and yours also. Such men deserve recognition.
-1 Corinthians 16:17,18

Day 2

Whatever you do, work at it with all your heart, as working for the Lord, not for men, since you know that you will receive an inheritance from the Lord as a reward. It is the Lord Christ you are serving.
-Colossians 3:23,24

Day 3

His master replied, "Well done, good and faithful servant! You have been faithful with a few things; I will put you in charge of many things. Come and share your master's happiness!" -Matthew 25:23

Day 4

In everything that he undertook in the service of God's temple and in obedience to the law and the commands, he sought his God and worked wholeheartedly. And so he prospered.   -2 Chronicles 31:21

Day 5

For it is not the one who commends himself who is approved, but the one whom the Lord commends.   -2 Corinthians 10:18

Reflections through the week

_____

_____

_____

_____

_____

_____

_____

_____

_____

_____

Week 42

Peace

Lord, "being at peace" is often talked about in this world but "being at peace" is rarely understood. Peace is the inner tranquility and calm of life that keeps the waters of my heart still while a storm rages outside me. Peace must replace worrying, anxious thoughts, overwhelmed feelings, fear, nervousness, or being upset. Today, when I am tempted to look at the storm around me, help me to turn my thinking toward the truth I find in You and Your Word. As I live in light of Your word I know that You will bring to me Your peace.

Day 1

You will keep in perfect peace him whose mind is steadfast, because he trusts in you. Trust in the LORD forever, for the LORD, is the Rock eternal. -Isaiah 26:3,4

Day 2

You have made known to me the path of life; you will fill me with joy in your presence, with eternal pleasures at your right hand.

-Psalm 16:11

Day 3

Peace I leave with you; my peace I give you. I do not give to you as the world gives. Do not let your hearts be troubled and do not be afraid.

-John 14:27

Day 4

"I have told you these things, so that in me you may have peace. In this world you will have trouble. But take heart! I have overcome the world."   -John 16:33

Day 5

And the peace of God, which transcends all understanding, will guard your hearts and your minds in Christ Jesus. Finally, brothers, whatever is true, whatever is noble, whatever is right, whatever is pure, whatever is lovely, whatever is admirable—if anything is excellent or praiseworthy—think about such things. Whatever you have learned or received or heard from me, or seen in me—put it into practice. And the God of peace will be with you.   -Philippians 4:7-9

Reflections through the week

_____

_____

_____

_____

_____

_____

_____

_____

_____

_____

_____

Week 43

Quiet

*Lord, "peace" has recently been my prayer. You are answer-
ing my prayer by enabling me to be at ease internally even
when there are storms. "Quiet" is when You choose to still
the storm. A break from the busyness of school makes the
personal storms in my life seem louder and my time occupied
with them is longer. Today, please still the storms in my life.
May the quiet that You bring allow me to rest safely with
You. If you choose not to still the storm, I choose today to
rest in Your peace—anyway!*

Day 1

And he said, Go forth, and stand upon the mount before the LORD.
And, behold, the LORD passed by, and a great and strong wind rent
the mountains, and brake in pieces the rocks before the LORD; but
the LORD was not in the wind: and after the wind an earthquake; but
the LORD was not in the earthquake: And after the earthquake a fire;
but the LORD was not in the fire: and after the fire a still small voice.
-1 Kings 19:11-12 (KJV)

Day 2

He (Jesus) got up, rebuked the wind and said to the waves, "Quiet!
Be still!" Then the wind died down and it was completely calm.
He said to his disciples, "Why are you so afraid? Do you still have no
faith?" They were terrified and asked each other, "Who is this?
Even the wind and the waves obey him!"   -Mark 4:39-41

Day 3

Make it your ambition to lead a quiet life, to mind your own business
and to work with your hands, just as we told you, so that your daily life
may win the respect of outsiders and so that you will not
be dependent on anybody.   -1 Thessalonians 4:11,12

Day 4

Better a dry crust with peace and quiet than a house full
of feasting, with strife.   -Proverbs 17:1

Day 5

Better one handful with tranquillity than two handfuls
with toil and chasing after the wind.   -Ecclesiastes 4:6

Reflections through the week

_____

_____

_____

_____

_____

_____

_____

_____

_____

_____

_____

Week 44

Rest

*Lord, the weekends during the school year and summer
breaks should be a time for rest for me. The weekends and
summers, however, are when all the work of home, family,
church and friends tumbles into my life. Rest is something
longed for, hoped for, yet rarely achieved. Rest is when
peace and quiet work in harmony to create a break in the
usual. Today, allow me to find rest or allow rest to find me.
Let me soak up the warmth of Your love while I rest in the
shade of Your protection.*

Day 1

Be still before the LORD and wait patiently for him; do not fret when
men succeed in their ways, when they carry out their wicked schemes.
-Psalm 37:7

Day 2

"Come to me, all you who are weary and burdened, and I will give you
rest. Take my yoke upon you and learn from me, for I am gentle and
humble in heart, and you will find rest for your souls. For my yoke is
easy and my burden is light."   -Matthew 11:28-30

Day 3

In vain you rise early and stay up late, toiling for food to eat—
for he grants sleep to those he loves.   -Psalm 127:2

Day 4

Therefore my heart is glad and my tongue rejoices; my body also will rest secure, because you will not abandon me to the grave, nor will you let your Holy One see decay. You have made known to me the path of life; you will fill me with joy in your presence, with eternal pleasures at your right hand.   -Psalm 16:9-11

Day 5

This then is how we know that we belong to the truth, and how we set our hearts at rest in his presence whenever our hearts condemn us. For God is greater than our hearts, and he knows everything. Dear friends, if our hearts do not condemn us, we have confidence before God and receive from him anything we ask, because we obey his commands and do what pleases him. And this is his command: to believe in the name of his Son, Jesus Christ, and to love one another as he commanded us. -1 John 3:19-23

Reflections through the week

_____

_____

_____

_____

_____

_____

_____

_____

_____

_____

Week 45

Remembrance

*Lord, I wonder what my students are doing during this break
from school? Are they growing forward or going backward in
character development and learning? What joys have they
experienced? What tragedies have occurred around them?
Are their families helping them to continue working through
life, building effective habits that will help them in the future?
So many questions, Lord, that I know and trust You are
answering. Today, I remember each one of my past students
and pray for their success both now and for eternity.*

Day 1

I thank my God every time I remember you. In all my prayers for all
of you, I always pray with joy because of your partnership in the gospel
from the first day until now, being confident of this, that he who
began a good work in you will carry it on to completion
until the day of Christ Jesus. -Phillipians 1:3-6

Day 2

And this is my prayer: that your love may abound more and more in
knowledge and depth of insight, so that you may be able to discern
what is best and may be pure and blameless until the day of Christ,
filled with the fruit of righteousness that comes through Jesus Christ—
to the glory and praise of God. -Phillipians 1:9-11

Day 3

For this reason, since the day we heard about you, we have not
stopped praying for you and asking God to fill you with the knowledge
of his will through all spiritual wisdom and understanding. And we
pray this in order that you may live a life worthy of the Lord and may
please him in every way: bearing fruit in every good work, growing in

the knowledge of God, being strengthened with all power according to his glorious might so that you may have great endurance and patience, and joyfully giving thanks to the Father, who has qualified you to share in the inheritance of the saints in the kingdom of light.

-Colossians 1:9-12

Day 4

We always thank God for all of you, mentioning you in our prayers. We continually remember before our God and Father your work produced by faith, your labor prompted by love, and your endurance inspired by hope in our Lord Jesus Christ.   -1 Thessalonians 1:2-3

Day 5

I thank God, whom I serve, as my forefathers did, with a clear conscience, as night and day I constantly remember you in my prayers. Recalling your tears, I long to see you, so that I may be filled with joy.

-1 Timothy 1:2,3

Reflections through the week

_____

_____

_____

_____

_____

_____

_____

_____

_____

_____

Week 46

Restoration

Lord, I know many teachers who enjoy antiques. The history behind each piece and how it has been restored captures their attention. It may be that a teacher by design is always seeking to help restore lives to function how You originally intended. Thank You for Your restoration work in my life. You have taken the long and patient approach to produce in me gifts and value that only You knew was there. Today, help me see in those I contact the hope of what they can be through Your restoration process.

Day 1

The LORD is my shepherd, I shall not be in want. He makes me lie down in green pastures, He leads me beside quiet water . He restores my soul. He guides me in paths of righteousness for His name's sake.
-Psalm 23:1-3

Day 2

Restore to me the joy of your salvation and grant me a willing spirit, to sustain me. Then I will teach transgressors your ways, and sinners will turn back to you.   -Psalm 51:12,13

Day 3

Restore us, O God; make your face shine upon us, that we may be saved. Restore us, O God Almighty; make your face shine upon us, that we may be saved.   -Psalm 80:3,7

Day 4

Restore us to yourself, O LORD, that we may return;
renew our days as of old. -Lamentations 5:21

Day 5

Humble yourselves, therefore, under God's mighty hand, that he may
lift you up in due time. Cast all your anxiety on him because he cares
for you. Be self-controlled and alert. Your enemy the devil prowls
around like a roaring lion looking for someone to devour. Resist him,
standing firm in the faith,   because you know that your brothers
throughout the world are undergoing the same kind of sufferings.
And the God of all grace, who called you to his eternal glory
in Christ, after you have suffered a little while,
will himself restore you and make you strong, firm and steadfast.
To him be the power for ever and ever. Amen.   -1 Peter 5:6-10

Reflections through the week

_____

_____

_____

_____

_____

_____

_____

_____

_____

_____

Week 47

Trust

Lord, who am I trusting? What am I trusting? Do I trust people, knowledge, money, things, history, science, health, experience, reasoning, etc.? Do I trust myself? The number of things worthy of trust seems to get smaller and smaller. This question of trust is an ancient struggle rooted in the core of every heart – including mine. Today, I reaffirm and refocus the energy of my life on trusting You, O Lord. While I do not understand all Your ways, I intentionally trust Your wisdom. May my trusting life teach others how to trust You.

Day 1

Trust in the LORD with all your heart and lean not on your own understanding; in all your ways acknowledge him, and he will make your paths straight.
-Proverbs 3:5,6

Day 2

This is what the LORD says: "Cursed is the one who trusts in man, who depends on flesh for his strength and whose heart turns away from the LORD. He will be like a bush in the wastelands; he will not see prosperity when it comes. He will dwell in the parched places of the desert, in a salt land where no one lives. "But blessed is the man who trusts in the LORD, whose confidence is in him. He will be like a tree planted by the water that sends out its roots by the stream. It does not fear when heat comes; its leaves are always green. It has no worries in a year of drought and never fails to bear fruit."
-Jeremiah 17:5-8

Day 3

My God is my rock, in whom I take refuge, my shield and the horn of my salvation. He is my stronghold, my refuge and my savior— from violent men you save me. I call to the LORD, who is worthy of praise, and I am saved from my enemies. -2 Samuel 22:3

Day 4

As for God, His way is perfect; the word of the LORD is flawless. He is a shield for all who take refuge in him. For who is God besides the LORD? And who is the Rock except our God? It is God who arms me with strength and makes my way perfect. He makes my feet like the feet of a deer; he enables me to stand on the heights. He trains my hands for battle; my arms can bend a bow of bronze. You give me your shield of victory; you stoop down to make me great. -2 Samuel 22:31-36

Day 5

But let all who take refuge in you be glad; let them ever sing for joy. Spread your protection over them, that those who love your name may rejoice in you. For surely, O LORD, you bless the righteous; you surround them with your favor as with a shield. -Psalm 5:11,12

Reflections through the week

Week 48

Habits

Lord, my life habits provide the daily structure for living. The simple habits like the morning and evening routine are maintained or changed when necessary. It is the habits of my heart that I find difficult to maintain or change. My habits reveal how I relate to others and how my thoughts control my actions. My habits have served me well in many ways, but there are always habits that need to be changed. Today, I am thankful for my good habits, but I need diligence to keep working on some habits of my heart that should change. Help me to see clearly those habits and enable me to find a strategy to replace poor habits with good ones.

Day 1

Trust in the LORD and do good;
dwell in the land and enjoy safe pasture. -Psalm 37:3

Day 2

"Whoever can be trusted with very little can also be trusted with much, and whoever is dishonest with very little will also be dishonest with much. So if you have not been trustworthy in handling worldly wealth, who will trust you with true riches? And if you have not been trustworthy with someone else's property, who will give you property of your own? -Luke 16:10-12

Day 3

Therefore, my dear brothers, stand firm. Let nothing move you. Always give yourselves fully to the work of the Lord, because you know that your labor in the Lord is not in vain. -1 Corinthians 15:58

Day 4

Do you not know that in a race all the runners run, but only one gets the prize?
Run in such a way as to get the prize. Everyone who competes in the games
goes into strict training. They do it to get a crown that will not last; but we do
it to get a crown that will last forever. Therefore I do not run like a man
running aimlessly; I do not fight like a man beating the air. No,
I beat my body and make it my slave so that after I have preached to others,
I myself will not be disqualified for the prize. -1 Corinthians 9:24-27

Day 5

Through these he has given us his very great and precious promises, so that
through them you may participate in the divine nature and escape the corrup-
tion in the world caused by evil desires. For this very reason, make every effort
to add to your faith goodness; and to goodness, knowledge; and to knowledge,
self-control; and to self-control, perseverance; and to perseverance, godliness;
and to godliness, brotherly kindness; and to brotherly kindness, love. For if
you possess these qualities in increasing measure, they will keep you from being
ineffective and unproductive in your knowledge of our Lord Jesus Christ.
-2 Peter 1:4-8

Reflections through the week

_____

_____

_____

_____

_____

_____

_____

_____

_____

Week 49

Delight

Lord, what satisfaction comes to my life when I find my delight in You. Delight is a combination of passionate energy and focused attention that I want to keep directed toward You. Delight is knowing that You are at work in my life through the wonder of Your powerful Word and the uniqueness of the people that You created. Today, may my energy and attention be kept on You, O Lord. May I hear Your voice, see Your hand, sense Your presence in all that I do. Please allow the people who see me today to be amazed at the energy and attention I am giving to You.

Day 1

Delight yourself in the Lord and
He will give you the desires of your heart. -Psalm 37:4

Day 2

Blessed is the man who does not walk in the counsel of the wicked or stand in the way of sinners or sit in the seat of mockers. But his delight is in the law of the LORD, and on his law he meditates day and night. He is like a tree planted by streams of water, which yields its fruit in season and whose leaf does not wither.
Whatever he does prospers. -Psalm 1:1-3

Day 3

I desire to do your will, O my God; your law is within my heart.
-Psalm 40:8

Day 4

O Lord, let your ear be attentive to the prayer of this your servant and
to the prayer of your servants who delight in revering your name.
Give your servant success today by granting him favor
in the presence of this man." -Nehemiah 1:11

Day 5

I said to the LORD, "You are my Lord; apart from you I have no good
thing." As for the saints who are in the land, they are the glorious
ones in whom is all my delight. The sorrows of those will increase
who run after other gods. I will not pour out their libations of blood or
take up their names on my lips. LORD, you have assigned me my
portion and my cup; you have made my lot secure.
The boundary lines have fallen for me in pleasant places;
surely I have a delightful inheritance. -Psalm 16:2

Reflections through the week

_____

_____

_____

_____

_____

_____

_____

_____

_____

_____

Week 50

Commitment

Lord, I've committed myself to teaching for another year. My time at home and away from the classroom has been a good diversion from the usual. There are questions that arise in my thinking about my commitment. Will I have the energy again to excel in my teaching? Will the students respond to my style? Do I continue to have the vision of hope for each life that I will touch? Today, I'm committed to You, Lord. Please answer my questions in a way that You think is best. Through my commitment to You and to teaching others, please accomplish Your work.

Day 1

Commit your way to the LORD; trust in him and he will do this: He will make your righteousness shine like the dawn, the justice of your cause like the noonday sun.   -Psalm 37:5,6

Day 2

To man belong the plans of the heart, but from the LORD comes the reply of the tongue. All a man's ways seem innocent to him, but motives are weighed by the LORD. Commit to the LORD whatever you do, and your plans will succeed.   -Proverbs 16:1-3

Day 3

So do not worry, saying, 'What shall we eat?' Or 'What shall we drink?' Or 'What shall we wear?' For the pagans run after all these things, and your heavenly Father knows that you need them. But seek first his kingdom and his righteousness, and all these things will be given to you as well. Therefore do not worry about tomorrow, for tomorrow will worry about itself. Each day has enough trouble of its own.   -Matthew 6:31-34

Day 4

So I reflected on all this and concluded that the righteous and the wise and what they do are in God's hands, but no man knows whether love or hate awaits him.   -Ecclesiastes 9:1

Day 5

And the things you have heard me say in the presence of many witnesses entrust to reliable men who will also be qualified to teach others.   -2 Timothy 2:2

Reflections through the week

_____

_____

_____

_____

_____

_____

_____

_____

_____

_____

Week 51

Waiting

Lord, the waiting that I encounter is similar to how a farmer plants his seed. He has the expected end in mind even while not knowing what weeds and pests he will need to fight or what weather or disaster might occur. My waiting is a resting trust that the quality seed I will sow in the lives of my students will produce the crop of truth lived out in lives that will endure weeds, pests, storms and disasters. Today, help me to wait patiently, believing that the vibrant seed of truth left in Your care will produce the results that You desire in the lives of Your students.

Day 1

Be still before the LORD and wait patiently for him; do not fret when men succeed in their ways, when they carry out their wicked schemes.

-Psalm 37:7

Day 2

"No good tree bears bad fruit, nor does a bad tree bear good fruit. Each tree is recognized by its own fruit. People do not pick figs from thornbushes, or grapes from briers. The good man brings good things out of the good stored up in his heart, and the evil man brings evil things out of the evil stored up in his heart. For out of the overflow of his heart his mouth speaks. -Luke 6:43-45

Day 3

Wait for the LORD; be strong and take heart and wait for the LORD.

-Psalm 27:14

Day 4

The LORD is good to those whose hope is in him, to the one who seeks him; it is good to wait quietly for the salvation of the LORD.

-Lamentations 3:25,26

Day 5

Let us not become weary in doing good, for at the proper time we will reap a harvest if we do not give up.   -Galatians 6:9

Reflections through the week

_____

_____

_____

_____

_____

_____

_____

_____

_____

_____

_____

Week 52

Finishing

Lord, a runner begins the race with a vision fixed on the finish line. That fixed attention must motivate, focus and dominate that runner's heart, soul and body during training and the race if he intends to finish well. Today, may I clearly see the finish line of my purpose in teaching. May I be motivated, focused, and dominated in my heart, soul, and body by the thought that above all else I am here on this earth to please You, O Lord. You are my Creator, Trainer, and Sustainer. Help me to begin well and help me to finish well!

Day 1

Do you not know that in a race all the runners run, but only one gets the prize? Run in such a way as to get the prize. Everyone who competes in the games goes into strict training. They do it to get a crown that will not last; but we do it to get a crown that will last forever. Therefore I do not run like a man running aimlessly; I do not fight like a man beating the air. No, I beat my body and make it my slave so that after I have preached to others, I myself will not be disqualified for the prize.
-1 Corinthians 9:24-27

Day 2

Brothers, I do not consider myself yet to have taken hold of it. But one thing I do: Forgetting what is behind and straining toward what is ahead, I press on toward the goal to win the prize for which God has called me heavenward in Christ Jesus.
-Philippians 3:13,14

Day 3

How great is the love the Father has lavished on us, that we should be called children of God! And that is what we are! The reason the world does not know us is that it did not know him. Dear friends, now we are children of God, and what we will be has not yet been made known. But we know that when he appears, we shall be like him, for we shall see him as he is. Everyone who has this hope in him purifies himself, just as he is pure. -1 John 3:1-3

Day 4

Therefore, since we are surrounded by such a great cloud of witnesses, let us throw off everything that hinders and the sin that so easily entangles, and let us run with perseverance the race marked out for us. Let us fix our eyes on Jesus, the author and perfecter of our faith, who for the joy set before him endured the cross, scorning its shame, and sat down at the right hand of the throne of God.   -Hebrews 12:1,2

Day 5

His master replied, 'Well done, good and faithful servant! You have been faithful with a few things; I will put you in charge of many things. Come and share your master's happiness!' For everyone who has will be given more, and he will have an abundance. Whoever does not have, even what he has will be taken from him.
-Matthew 25:23,29

Reflections through the week

_____

_____

_____

_____

_____

_____

_____

_____

_____

_____

Scripture Index

Order Form

Fax Orders: (765) 457-0662 **Telephone Orders:** (765) 457-0662
Postal Orders: Providence Publications, P.O. Box 882
                      Kokomo, IN 46903-0882
Internet Orders: www.providencepubl.com

E-mail: info@providencepubl.com

Person Ordering:_____

Title: _____

Organization: _____

Address: _____ State: ___ Zip: _____

Telephone: (___)___-_____ Fax: (___)___-_____

E-Mail Address: _____

The Teacher's Daily Helper

Pricing:
1-4 copies $9.95
5-11 copies $8.75
12 or more copies $7.50

	Qty.	Price Each	Total
	#	**$**	**$**
Indiana Residents add 5% Sales Tax			**$**
Shipping & Handling			**$**
TOTAL			**$**

Shipping:
First copy $2.75
2-4 copies $4.25
5-11 copies $5.75
12 or more copies 10% of total order amount

Payment:
Checks or Money Orders payable to: PROVIDENCE PUBLICATIONS

VISA   MasterCard   VISA/MC Card #: _____

Exp. Date ___/___ Name on card: _____

Signature: _____ Date: _____